MW00873157

THIS NOTEBOOK BELONGS TO:

Made in United States
North Haven, CT
14 July 2023

38986951R00083